The Ghostly Tales of Northeast South Dakota

Published by Arcadia Children's Books
A Division of Arcadia Publishing, Inc.
Charleston, SC
www.arcadiapublishing.com

First published 2025
Manufactured in the United States

Designed by Jessica Nevins
Images used courtesy of Shutterstock.com.

ISBN: 9781467197915
Library of Congress Control Number: 2024950551

Spooky America

The Ghostly Tales of Northeast South Dakota

Anna Lardinois

Adapted from *Ghosts and Legends of Northeast South Dakota* by Deborah Cuyle

NORTH DAKOTA

7

6

1

2

3

5

SOUTH DAKOTA

4

NEBRASKA

COLORADO

KANSAS

Table of Contents & Map Key

Minnesota

Iowa

Missouri

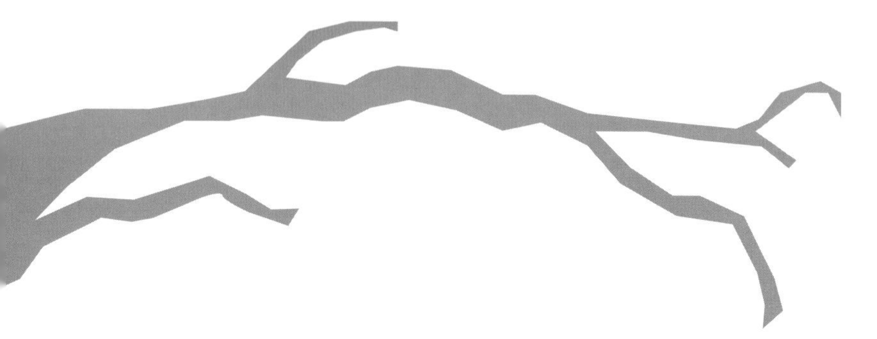

Foreword

Northeast South Dakota is known for more than its sprawling farmland and beautiful lakes . . . it is also a very haunted section of the state! Several ghosts call Fort Sisseton their forever home, while some local universities also house a few restless spirits. Spooks roam local cemeteries, a male spirit comes back from the dead to haunt his wife, and unearthed skulls frighten road workers! There have even been sightings of a local monster similar to Bigfoot that roams the land.

Explore these scary locales adapted from my book, *Ghosts and Legends of Northeast South Dakota*, through writer Anna Lardinois, as she winds through these spooky tales that date as far back as the late 1800s! So, cuddle up with some hot cocoa and discover some of South Dakota's creepiest legends and spookiest tales in *The Ghostly Tales of Northeast South Dakota*!

—Deborah Cuyle, author of
Ghosts and Legends of Northeast South Dakota

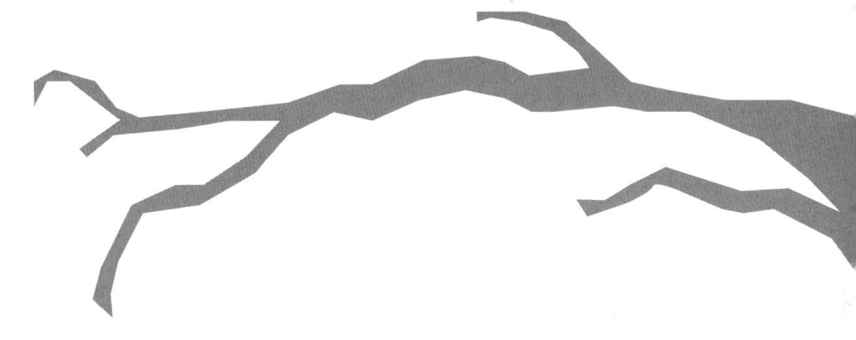

Welcome to Spooky Northeast South Dakota!

Let's explore the spooky side of South Dakota together. South Dakota is bordered by North Dakota in the north, Minnesota and Iowa in the east, Nebraska in the south, and Wyoming and Montana in the west.

The word Dakota is a Native American Sioux word that means "friendly" or "allies." South Dakota is called The Mount Rushmore State because of the enormous sculpture of former U.S. presidents carved into the Black Hills in Southwest South Dakota. The faces of George Washington, Abraham Lincoln, Thomas Jefferson, and Theodore Roosevelt are an amazing sixty feet tall! Believe it or not, almost three million people a year visit this famous landmark!

You may have also heard South Dakota referred to as the Coyote State. The state animal is the coyote, and it is estimated there are about 75,000 coyotes in South Dakota—that's one coyote per square mile. Now, that's a howlingly good fact!

South Dakota became the fortieth state in 1889, but there have been ghosts here for as long as people have lived on the land. In this book, we'll explore some of northeast South Dakota's most haunted sites. From the restless spirits that remain at Fort Sisseton Historic State Park to the legendary Taku-He that roams the forests near Little Eagle, you're about to meet South Dakota's spookiest specters.

Are you ready to discover South Dakota's most *spooktacular* ghosts? Turn the page . . . if you dare!

Scenic South Dakota

Frightening Old Fort Sisseton

Old Fort Sisseton has a reputation as one of the spookiest places in northeast South Dakota. If you believe the tales—and there are plenty of them—that place is FULL of ghosts!

Before you meet the specters that call Fort Sisseton home, you should know the fort is the oldest building in northeast South Dakota. It was established around 1864 as a frontier army post as the country pushed westward. Originally named Fort Wadsworth after Brigadier General Samuel Wadsworth, the fort was built to protect the early settlers. In 1876, the name of the fort was changed to Fort Sisseton. That name came from the Sisseton Wahpeton Oyate, members of the Santee Dakota nation who lived in the area. Today, the grounds are called Fort Sisseton Historic State Park. It's a great place to learn about South Dakota history. And, if you're lucky (or very unlucky, depending how you look at it), it is also a great place to see ghosts!

Legend has it there are three very active ghosts on the land. The first is an apparition that many call The Lady in White.

This mysterious specter is always seen wearing a long and flowing white nightgown. Those who have seen her say it looks like the kind of nightgown that would have been worn in the mid-1800s. She can be seen through the upstairs windows of a house on the property. She carries a candle in her hand as she walks from room to room on the second floor.

If the vision of the eerie lady walking in the ghostly glow of a candle from another realm doesn't scare you, maybe this will. Many believe The Lady in White is using her otherworldly candle to burn bedbugs! Yes,

bedbugs: those tiny bugs about the size and color of an apple seed that come out at night to bite you and drink your blood!

This probably needs an explanation. We know that during the 1870s, the fort was infested with bedbugs. Unlike today, there were not many ways to get rid of bedbugs at the time. One sure way to kill the little bloodsuckers was to burn them to death.

At night, when the bedbugs would show themselves, the women who worked at the fort would take their candles and burn the bugs off the walls. They would hold the candle very close to the wall so the heat from the flame would kill the bugs. The workers would kill THOUSANDS of these horrible bugs every night.

Once the dead bugs

fell to the floor, the women would sweep up dustpans filled with their burnt carcasses. They did this for years until they were able to get the infestation under control.

The bedbugs are long gone, but The Lady in White remains. No one knows the identity of this mystery lady in the nightgown or why, from beyond the grave, she continues her grim task of ridding the fort of bedbugs. But if you peer into the house's windows after the sun sets, you just might catch her carrying out this unpleasant nightly chore.

The Lady in White is not the only spirit who has decided to spend the afterlife at the old fort. She is joined by the ghost of a lively little boy. This unknown boy likes to play with the children who visit the property. Not only can he be seen, he is also able to make physical contact with the living. Visitors report that he tugs on their clothing to try to get their attention.

Well, this nameless boy certainly has my attention! How about yours? If a strange, silent boy tugged on your pant leg, what would you do?

You can think about that question while you meet the third ghost that has made the fort its home.

"When I was visiting Fort Sisseton, I felt as though I was being watched all the time, but no one was there," Mike D., a visitor to the park, told a ghostly researcher. "I have heard many rumors of the fort being haunted by an old soldier. I wondered who this soldier was. Did he die on the property? I did not actually see the ghost soldier, but I certainly felt the hair on the back of my neck stand up a few times for no reason!"

Mike D. is correct. There IS a ghostly soldier haunting the grounds, but he did not die on the property. Meet soldier J.C. Smith.

This soldier was part of a well-known group of African American soldiers known as the Buffalo Soldiers. He served in the Company D Twenty-Fifth Regiment Colored Infantry.

He worked on many of the buildings still standing on the property. If you visit today, you can see where Smith carved his name on a wall in the guardhouse, a building he helped construct. Records show that Smith served at the fort between 1864 and 1865.

No one knows why Smith's spirit remains at the old fort. Some think he scratched his name on the guardhouse wall because he always planned to return to the fort in the afterlife.

It is said that Smith's apparition likes to tap on the shoulders of the living to get their attention. If you long for your own ghostly encounter with the soldier, he is most often seen near the old pay phone on the property.

While these three ghosts might be the best-known spirits to haunt Fort Sisseton, they probably aren't the only ones. Visitors report seeing strange lights, being touched by unseen hands, and observing ghostly figures.

There doesn't seem to be a question about whether or not the old fort is haunted—that seems clear. The question that remains is *why* is it haunted? What remains that attracts the dead?

On second thought, maybe it's safer to let the answer to that question remain unknown.

Old Fort Sisseton

The Tale of the Throndson Sisters

Have you ever been caught in a blizzard?

I'm not talking about a snowstorm—I mean a *real* blizzard with air so cold it takes your breath away and blowing snow that blinds you. If you have, then you understand the power and danger of a winter storm.

If you haven't, you can only imagine how easy it is to get confused when so much snow swirls around you that you can't even see your own feet!

The Throndson family experienced that kind of winter storm on January 6, 1903, when a blizzard blew into the town of Sisseton on the Coteau des Prairies.

It was a storm that changed their lives forever. The Throndsons were a Norwegian immigrant family of homesteaders. The parents, Knut and Caroline, had five children.

The January day started out cold but sunny. Looking out the window, Knut decided it was a good day to visit the nearby homestead of another Norwegian family, Tobias and Bertha Herigstad.

Caroline decided to stay behind to take care of their three younger children, but Knut brought along his two older daughters, Menne, age fifteen, and Theoline, age thirteen. The trio hitched their horses to their sled and set off, laughing and chatting as they glided over the snow. They didn't have far to travel. The Herigstads only lived about a quarter of a mile away, or about a five-minute walk when there was no snow.

The family had a pleasant afternoon visiting with their neighbors. Soon, the sun began to set, and it was time to head home. But just as the Throndsons left the Herigstads' homestead, storm clouds rolled in. They put their heads down to shield themselves from the icy blasts of wind that signaled the start of the storm.

Knut and his daughters huddled together in the sled to stay warm as the snow swirled around them. Within moments, Knut was blinded by the white-out storm. He held the

reins tightly in his hands and hoped the horses had a better view of where the sled was headed.

The frigid wind burned the girls' cheeks as a blizzard raged around them. The sled moved forward as the horses slowly trotted through the growing snow drifts. Suddenly, all three Throndsons lurched forward and the sound of splintering wood rose above the howl of the wind.

Their sled had struck a rock hidden beneath the snow. The horses were still as Knut got out

of the sled to examine the damage. He saw that one of the sled's runners was broken. The sled was of no use to them now. Knut tried to judge the distance to their home, but all he could see was the snow that continued to fall. He knew they had to keep moving or he and his daughters might freeze to death in the storm.

Knut came up with a plan. He told Menne and Theoline to grab the tails of the horses and hold on tightly. He then took the reins in his

hands and led the horses through the storm.

Knut moved forward through the storm. He could not see or hear the girls, but he knew as long as the girls kept their hands grasped firmly around the horses' tails, they would not be lost in the storm.

Together, the family fought through the storm, step by step. The wind was strong, and the snow was blinding, but Knut continued to move forward. He was determined they would make it home. Finally, after what felt like forever, Knut saw the glow of a candle in a window! At last! They were safely home.

Or, at least, that is what Knut thought.

When he turned around to let his daughters know they were home, the girls were gone.

His heart sank. Where could they be? Without thinking twice, he ran back into the storm, calling their names over and over. Knut and his neighbor Tobias searched for the girls all night long, but the storm made it impossible to see, and their voices could not be heard over the howling winds.

When morning finally came, the storm had passed. Knut went back outside to look for the girls. Snow covered everything around him. There was not a trace of footsteps in the snow. He shouted the names of his daughters into the cold, still air. There was no response.

He began to walk in the direction of the Herigstads' home, continuing to call for the girls, but all he could hear was the echo of his own voice.

As he approached his neighbors' farm, he noticed what appeared to be two bundles on the ground. When he walked toward the bundles, he recognized the cloak of his younger daughter. He could feel his heart begin to break. He'd found his girls, but he was too late. Menne and Theoline were dead.

The frozen girls were found close to the Herigstad home. So close that if they had not been blinded by the storm, they could have easily made it to safety. But that was not their fate.

People on the prairie still remember the story of the two sisters. Many believe the spirits of Menne and Theoline still linger on the Coteau des Prairies. The ghostly girls are said to help those who find themselves lost in the snow and gently guide stranded travelers toward safety.

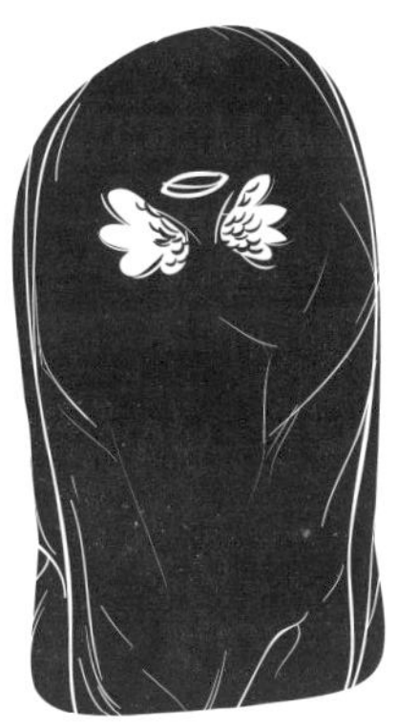
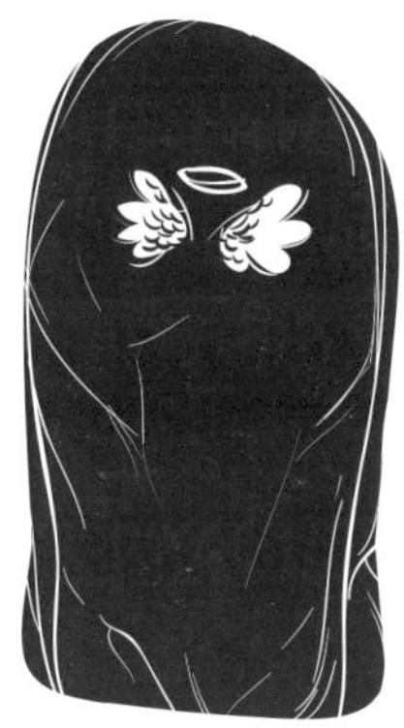

Over the last one hundred years, a surprising number of people have told stories of being rescued by what they describe as an "unknown force." The force remains with the travelers until they reach safety. Interestingly, this force always seems to guide the lost in the direction of the Herigstad homestead.

It has been said that in the years that followed, the Herigstad family always opened their doors to anyone who needed shelter. They wanted to be sure no one else faced the same fate as the two lost sisters.

Do Menne and Theoline still remain in the earthly realm to protect lost travelers? That's hard to say, but if you ever find yourself trapped in a blizzard on the prairie, I bet you'll hope the legend of these spectral sisters is not a legend after all!

CHAPTER 3

Spine-Tingling Schools

Legend has it that both Northern State University in Aberdeen and South Dakota State University in Brookings are haunted! The spooky spirits that linger on these campuses have frightened generations of students and show no signs of moving on.

Let's meet a few of these ghosts! First up are the spirits that haunt Northern State University.

For fifty years, the students who lived in the Jerde Hall dormitory on campus reported strange happenings, particularly students who stayed on the fourth floor of the building. Here, students often reported a spine-chilling sight. It wasn't a spooky shadow or a creepy figure—it was the ghost of a little girl!

The otherworldly child would appear out of nowhere, running up and down the hallways. Some students even woke up to find her standing at the end of their beds. As the students trembled in fear under their covers, the ghostly girl would softly whisper, "Shh . . . " followed by a giggle.

Some students swore they spotted her reflection in mirrors throughout the building. Imagine brushing your hair in front of a mirror and catching a glimpse of a small, smiling girl behind you. When you turned around to speak to the girl, you would find yourself in the room alone. That is the very experience many students had while living in Jerde Hall!

No one knew who this little girl was or why she haunted Jerde Hall. Where did she come from? What was she doing there? It was a mystery that no one could solve. But one thing was certain: she loved playing tricks and sneaking around the old dorm.

In 2018, Jerde Hall was torn down. The university transferred the property on which it once stood to the South Dakota School for the Blind and Visually Impaired. Since then, no one has reported seeing the little ghost girl. Did she disappear with the old building, or has she found a new home on the campus of Northern State? Only time will tell if the ghostly girl has found a new building to haunt.

Even though Jerde Hall is gone, there's another spooky place on campus: the Johnson Fine Arts Center. Built in the 1970s, this building has its own ghostly visitor—a man who likes to whistle as he walks through the halls.

Many believe this ghost might have been someone who worked at the school a long time ago, who just didn't want to leave. This mischievous ghost likes to flick the lights on and off in the building. People think he may have been employed by the school because in empty hallways there have been reports of the sound of keys jingling, just like the ones a janitor might carry. Perhaps this spirit is simply continuing the job he did in life from beyond the grave?

Students and staff are not afraid of the spirit who haunts the Johnson Fine Arts Center. Those who have encountered him do not find him scary. Instead, he is thought to be a playful spirit who just enjoys hanging around the place he loved.

The spirit who has made South Dakota State University its home is a bit more active than those on the Northern State University campus.

South Dakota State has a music-loving entity that has made its home in the Doner Auditorium. This ghost makes his presence known in several ways. This spirit likes to turn lights on and off and play the theater's organ.

Just imagine walking past the auditorium

at night and hearing organ music coming from the dark and vacant building. It's enough to make the hairs on the neck stand up!

Some believe this musical spirit is that of a janitor who fell to his death from a balcony in

the auditorium in 1919. The ghost has become part of campus lore. Students have named the spirit George. It is believed George dwells in a room hidden behind a staircase in the building.

I wonder how many brave—or foolish, depending on your thoughts about ghosts—students have searched for George's secret room?

What do you think? Would you go to a school you knew was haunted? If you did, would you try to find the ghosts—or would you stay far away? I know what I'd do. I'd stay as far away as I could!

South Dakota State University

Dr. Mitchel's Strange Night in the Grand House

Even as a child, F.A. Mitchel was a little odd. The boy claimed he could read the thoughts of the person sitting next to him. He found his ability to do this *fascinating*. It led Mitchel to read anything he could get his hands on that explained how the human brain and body worked.

All that research paid off. Mitchel eventually grew up and became a doctor.

In 1914, Dr. Mitchel decided to take a small vacation. He needed a break from the demands of his job. He left his home in Sisseton and kept traveling until he found a quiet boardinghouse on the side of the road.

Mitchel was tired and the boarding house looked like the perfect place to get a good night's sleep. He rented a room for a few nights.

His stay was just as peaceful as he had hoped it would be. The doctor got into the habit of sitting on the porch each evening and watching the sun set. As the sky grew darker, Mitchel would look across the sprawling yard and admire the home just up the road from the boardinghouse.

It was a fine old home. He was impressed with the grand pillars that lined the porch. The doctor thought it was the finest home in the area, and he enjoyed looking at it as part of his relaxing evening routine.

One night, long after the sun had gone down, the doctor was in his rented room getting ready to go to bed. Just before he was set to change into his pajamas, he heard what sounded like a carriage arrive at the front of the boardinghouse.

Before he could wonder who might have arrived at that time of night, he heard a panicked voice shouting, "Doctor? Are you a doctor?!"

Dr. Mitchel quickly opened the window in his room and leaned out to get a better look at who was calling for him. He saw a nervous-looking man pacing in the yard.

"What's the matter?" Mitchel called out to the man.

"Quick, come with me!" was all the stranger managed to say.

The doctor pulled on his jacket and grabbed his medical bag. He ran down the stairs and quickly climbed into the man's carriage. Mitchel tried to get the man to tell him what was wrong as they rode into the darkness, but the stranger just stared ahead with the reins of the carriage clutched tightly in his fists.

Within moments, they were in front of the fine home with the large pillars that the doctor knew so well from his nights relaxing on the porch of the boardinghouse. The doctor

climbed out of the carriage and followed the man into the house that he had spent so much time admiring.

As the men walked through the doorway of the home, the doctor said, "This is the very house I have so often admired and dreamed of." The stranger did not respond, but the doctor did not notice. His attention was drawn to the woman standing in the foyer.

She was a lovely young woman finely dressed in lace and bows. She seemed upset, but the doctor could not tell what was wrong. Before he could ask her, the woman said, "Come with me," and then headed up a grand staircase.

When they reached the top of the stairs, the woman stopped in front of a closed door. She slowly turned the glass doorknob, and the heavy door creaked open. The doctor peered through the doorway into the darkened room.

It was a bedroom. A frail-looking woman was lying on a grand four-poster bed in the dim room. A man sat at the woman's bedside, holding one of her hands, while a young girl stood on the opposite side of the bed, clasping the other.

The doctor stepped into the room and walked toward the bed. He gently moved the bedsheets to get a better look at the woman. Even in the dim light, he saw the sheets were soaked in blood. He noticed someone had clumsily attempted to bandage the woman's wounds before he arrived, but fresh blood continued to seep from beneath the bandages.

Looking at the pale woman and the amount of blood she had already lost, the doctor feared she was too near death to save. He reached into his bag to grab some fresh gauze to rebandage her wounds.

Before he could cut the first piece of gauze,

though, the woman began to gasp for air. The doctor put down the bandage. He knew death would soon take her.

As the woman wheezed, she turned to the man sitting at her bedside.

"Are you convinced of the unjustness of your suspicions?" she whispered.

The doctor stood quietly at the foot of the dying woman's bed. He was puzzled by her words. But the man next to her seemed to understand exactly what she meant.

"Yes, yes. Forgive me," the man said in a voice heavy with grief.

With her final breath, the woman replied, "I forgive you. Goodbye." And with that, she died.

The doctor had been in the presence of death many times. He quietly gathered his things and slipped out of the bedroom. He knew there was nothing left to do but let the family mourn the loss of the woman in private.

As he walked down the grand staircase, he saw people beginning to gather in the parlor of the great home. That was not unusual. It is common for people to come together to grieve the loss of a life. What he thought was strange was the way the people in the parlor looked.

It seemed as if everyone was wearing costumes. They wore old clothes that had not been stylish in a very long time. It looked like a gathering of early South Dakota settlers. The doctor's modern clothing seemed out of place among the old-fashioned neck ties of the men and the long, full skirts and petticoats worn by the women.

Confused, the doctor made his way out of the house. He saw the man who had brought him from the boardinghouse leaning against a pillar on the porch. Without a word, the man walked toward the carriage. He motioned the doctor to follow him.

Mitchel climbed into the carriage. The doctor heard nothing but the rhythmic clatter of the horse's hooves on the gravel as the pair rode through the night in silence.

When the carriage arrived at the boardinghouse, the doctor wished the man a good night and entered the house. He was exhausted. He wearily climbed the stairs to his room and soon fell into a deep sleep.

When he awoke the next morning, Mitchel

was unsettled. He thought about the events of the night before. His mind was filled with questions. Who was the woman who had died and what had happened to her? Why had everyone in the home been dressed so strangely? And why did he feel like something was very wrong?

Determined to find answers, the doctor got

dressed and joined the other boardinghouse guests in the parlor downstairs.

As he began to recount the events of the night before, he noticed the guests exchanging bewildered looks. None of them had heard a carriage pull up, or a man shouting for a doctor. It seemed they thought it was odd that they had all slept through the commotion in the front yard.

The doctor shrugged and continued his story. But when he said that the carriage had taken him to the nearby grand home with pillars, the owner of the boardinghouse interrupted.

"That's impossible," the owner said. "No one has lived in that home for over thirty years!"

The doctor felt a shiver of fear run down his spine. How could that be? He had just been in the home. He'd seen the family inside and witnessed a woman die. It had all been real. *Hadn't* it?

The doctor, who had suspected since childhood that he had otherworldly abilities, started to suspect he had experienced something supernatural that night. He decided to investigate the home in search of answers. He had to figure out what had happened.

He soon uncovered a story about the home from many years ago. He learned that a wealthy family had once lived in the grand home. The lady of the house was married to jealous, angry man. Her husband convinced himself that the lady had not been true to him. His anger grew as he thought about the imagined love affair.

Overcome with jealousy, the man plunged a

knife into his wife. He stabbed her again and again until he regained control of himself. Shocked by what he had done, he carried his bloodied wife to the bed they shared. Moments later, she died.

When the doctor realized what had happened in the house so long ago, he concluded that somehow, some way, he had been transported back in time to the night of the woman's murder! People who heard the doctor's story thought he had just experienced a vivid dream rather than a true paranormal event, but the doctor did not agree.

In fact, he was so certain he had stepped into the past that he risked his reputation and his medical practice by sharing the story of that strange night to anyone who would listen to him.

Those who believe his tale often wonder if

the murdered woman somehow orchestrated these otherworldly events to make sure the world knew she was murdered, and that her husband was her killer.

What do you think? Did Mitchel travel back in time to witness the death of a murdered woman, or was it all a dream? And, if it really

was a dream, how could he have known about the tragic events that occurred in the abandoned home so many years earlier?

Either way, this is one seriously spooky tale!

The Creepy Milbank Cemetery

Is the Milbank Cemetery haunted? Paranormal enthusiast Beth W. is certain of it.

"I often wander cemeteries. I find them fascinating. I just love the old tombstones," she told a paranormal researcher collecting ghost stories. "One time, I was wandering around the Milbank Cemetery, and I saw what appeared to be a man standing next to a grave. I did not see any other cars, so I figured he possibly walked there. But as quickly as he appeared, he disappeared! It startled me. I knew I had just seen a ghost!"

Beth is not the only one who has had an otherworldly experience in the cemetery. Many people have reported seeing the ghostly apparition of a man roaming the property.

Those who have seen him state that this spirit appears to be confused as he moves between the tombstones.

He is thought to be the ghost of a man who met his untimely demise in 1912.

You might know that South Dakota was a dangerous place in the early 1900s. There were few police officers and plenty of trains to jump on to get far away from the scene of any crime committed. Just like most towns along the rail lines, when train tracks came to Milbank, the town became more violent and lawless.

No one in town was terribly surprised when the bloody corpse of a murdered man was discovered on top of a passenger train car one hot summer night in 1912.

A night operator in Ortonville noticed something strange on the top of the train as it pulled out of the station. The next stop along the route was ten miles away in Milbank. So, the operator alerted the upcoming train depot dispatcher to stop the train and investigate what he saw.

When the train pulled into the depot, officers were already on the scene. As soon as the train made a complete stop, Officer Derrick climbed up to the train's roof. He instantly spotted the body. As he moved closer, he could see it was a dead man. His body was covered in blood, and he appeared to have a gash in his neck.

Justice A.J. Bleser was called down to the train depot to help with the dead man. When he arrived, Bleser and Derrick examined the corpse together. They discovered the man's throat had been slit.

Despite the body that had been discovered on the roof of the train, the train's conductor was eager to stay on schedule. He pressured the Milbank authorities to remove the body from the passenger car and allow the train to continue its route.

Bleser and Derrick managed to get the body off the roof. They decided to store the deceased in the baggage room at the train depot until they could find a more suitable location for the man. Now that the corpse was off the train, they concluded the man had not been dead for long. The body was still warm and the slash in his neck was still dripping with blood.

The men searched the pockets of the corpse

in hopes of finding something that might identify him. They didn't find much. The man had a few dollars in his pockets, a newspaper, a few notes on scraps of paper, and an envelope with "Fred Kirchbaum of Granite Falls, Minnesota" written on it.

When the sun rose, workers along the railroad tracks spotted blood alongside the railroad tracks in Correll, Minnesota. Upon closer inspection, they also found a bloody hat nearby. They felt certain Correll was the scene of the crime, but they still had no idea the name of the dead man.

The Correll police looked over the notes in

the man's pocket and eventually discovered that the dead man's name was Edward Riley.

Officials also tracked down Fred Kirchbaum, the man whose name was found on the envelope in Riley's pocket. Kirchbaum, it turned out, was a farmer Riley had worked for just for a few days. The farmer didn't know much about the man. He only knew the dead man's name was Ed and that he was a hard worker and good person.

Kirchbaum told the police the last time he saw Ed, the man mentioned he was headed to Granite Falls, Minnesota in search of a job. If he couldn't get work there, his plan was to head to Milbank to find a job.

That is where the trail goes cold. Police never discovered who killed Riley or how he ended up on the roof of the train. Despite having the man's name, the authorities could not find any of Riley's family members. No one who knew the man knew he was dead, and there was no one to claim Ed Riley's body.

Eventually, the body needed to be laid to rest somewhere. That somewhere turned out to be Milbank Cemetery.

With no one to mourn him, the local reverend said a short prayer at the grave of the unclaimed man, and he was quickly buried.

Yet, that is not the end of Ed Riley's story. But you already knew that.

Ed Riley's restless spirit still wanders the old Milbank Cemetery. Some believe the man's sudden and violent death may be the reason he remains on this side of the earthly veil. They think Ed Riley is trapped in this realm and needs help to move into the light that will take him into the other world.

Poor Ed Riley! Perhaps someday Ed might find his way to the other side, but for now, he remains on the cemetery grounds looking for something he has yet to find.

I Love You to Death

Can the dead seek revenge from beyond the grave? Before you answer that question, you might want to read about the strange events that happened in Watertown in 1910.

It begins when a man named Phillip Hartman began courting a woman named Fanny.

People around town thought the couple was an odd pairing. Fanny was a few years older than Phillip, and she had a very plain face. She was nothing like the other girls Phillip had taken on dates. But Fanny was from a very wealthy family. Townspeople assumed Phillip found Fanny's money more important than her looks.

People gossiped about the couple, but Fanny ignored all their comments. She loved Phillip, and she believed he loved her for who she was, not for her money. Before long, the mismatched couple married.

They lived happily as man and wife for nearly two years when tragedy struck. Fanny suddenly became very sick. Those who visited the woman's bedside murmured that it appeared she had been poisoned.

But, of course, there was no evidence of this. Fanny grew more ill, and within days, it was clear she wouldn't recover from this mysterious malady.

Fanny summoned the last of her strength and called her husband to her bedside. She was so weak, she could not speak above a whisper. Phillip leaned over the bed and put his head near Fanny's mouth so he could hear what she wanted to tell him. He was so close he could feel her ragged breath on his cheek as she struggled to get the words out.

"Phil, I am going to leave you soon," she said between gasps. "Remember, if you marry again, I swear, I will haunt you. I will never let another woman have you! Now kiss me, darling."

Phillip did as she asked. Her lips were cold against his. When he pulled away, he knew Fanny was gone.

A doctor came to confirm Fanny was dead. Then, Phillip began to make arrangements to lay his wife to rest. It was a lovely funeral, and the townspeople could see that the man was truly heartbroken over the loss.

For at least a year, Phillip mourned Fanny's death. His friends and family tried to cheer him

up, but it was no use. He kept to himself while he struggled in sadness.

It took some time, but eventually Phillip started to feel better. Once again, he met with friends and socialized with townspeople. That was how he met Amelle Kinkaid.

When Phillip first laid eyes on Amelle, he felt like he had been struck by lightning! He was instantly smitten. She was charming, beautiful, and young—just like the women he courted before he met his wife, Fanny.

He fell in love with Amelle, but Fanny was still on his mind. He remembered the promise he'd made to her on her deathbed. He knew Fanny would seethe with jealousy if she were still alive. Amelle was everything Fanny was not, and Phillip knew his late wife would hate to know he was courting the lovely young woman.

But, Phillip reasoned, Fanny was dead. What she felt and the promise that he made her no longer mattered. Fanny was in her grave, and he was free to live his life as he wanted. At least, that is what he believed when he asked Amelle to marry him.

Amelle and Phillip were married, and soon after, Phillip received a job offer that would take the newlyweds to California. Phillip accepted the job. He was eager to begin a new life with his new bride. So, they packed up their belongings and left Watertown for sunny California.

It only took a few weeks for their fortunes to change.

Phillip was struck with a stomachache so painful that he was forced into his bed. Day after day, the pain grew worse. The mystery illness was strangely similar to the one that had killed Fanny. Amelle stayed by her new husband's side, tending to him day and night. But instead of getting better, Phillip's sickness got worse.

After four days at his bedside, Amelle noticed that Phillip was looking slightly better. He had a bit of color in his cheeks, and his breathing was less ragged than it had been the day before. She looked at her sleeping husband with relief. She thought the worst of the illness was over. Exhausted from days of caring for Phillip, she thought it was safe to leave his bedside and take a quick nap before he awoke.

She left Phillip's room and curled up under a quilt on the couch in the parlor. She closed her eyes, and just as she was about to drift off into sleep, she saw something that made her scream in terror. The ghost of Fanny appeared before her!

She leaped off the couch and ran back to Phillip's room as fast as her frightened legs would carry her. Then Amelle threw open the door, tears streaming down her face, and screeched, "Phillip! Phillip! Fanny is after me! She has come to take you. She says that I have had you long enough, and now she is going to have you for herself. But I will not give you up. I will not!"

Phillip stared at his trembling second wife. He sat up in bed and tried to console her.

"Calm down, Amelle. This is all nonsense," Phillip said in a soothing voice.

"No, it is not!" Amelle protested. "I saw her as distinctly as I see you now. I know it is her from her picture. She had on a brown dress, and she was furious. 'He is my husband, not yours,' she told me. 'You have had him long enough,' she said, pointing her finger at me! 'Now I mean to take him as I said I would.' Tell me, Phillip, did she ever say such a thing to you?"

Phillip listened to Amelle's words carefully. Goosebumps formed on his arms and he felt a shiver run down his spine. He knew in an instant that Fanny had returned from the grave.

Despite his fear, he tried to reason with himself. He told himself that Fanny was dead. It was impossible for her to have anything to do with the world of the living. Wasn't it?

Phillip did not want to worry Amelle, so he lied to her and said, "No, no. Of course not! Such things are just folly. Here, lie down here on the bed, and I will fetch you a nice glass of wine."

Amelle climbed into the bed Phillip had just left and slipped beneath the covers. She closed her eyes and tried to get control of herself. As she calmed down, she told herself that ghosts were not real and that what she'd experienced had just been a dream.

Amelle opened her eyes and saw Phillip standing as still as a statue just outside the doorway of the bedroom. As she looked at him, he suddenly began gasping for air. A gurgling sound came from somewhere deep in his throat, as if he were being choked. He flailed his arms in front of him. It was as if Phillip was trying to fight off an invisible attacker.

Frozen in fear, Amelle watched as Phillip fell to the floor. She rushed to his side and held the dying man's hand into her own as he hissed out his final word: "*Fanny!*"

Amelle shuddered as she stared at the face of her now-dead husband. It hadn't been a dream, Amelle knew it. Fanny had been in the house and taken back what Amella had claimed as her own. Fanny and Phillip were reunited. But it is anyone's guess if the pair rested peacefully after Fanny pulled him into the afterlife. It's not likely, if you ask me.

Now that you've heard the story of Phillip and Fanny, I'll ask you again—can the dead seek revenge from beyond the grave?

The Ghostly Children of Red Iron Lake

What do you think happens if you disturb the final resting place of a body? Some say the spirit of the body in the grave becomes restless and begins to roam the earth, seeking the peace of eternal rest.

What if the grave in question contains *five* bodies? Do you think that somehow makes this worse?

Read on, because that is just what happened back in the fall of 1922 near Red Iron Lake.

One day, workers were doing some construction work near State Highway 10. One of the workers dug into the earth with the tip of his shovel. He struck something but didn't know what it was. It was definitely hard, but it didn't feel like a rock. The worker carefully dug a little deeper. And then he saw it. He'd uncovered a bone—a human bone!

The workers gathered around the hole to gape at the bone sticking up from the ground. They could see what appeared to be a skull just beneath the surface of the dirt. The men

dropped their shovels. They had no idea what they'd discovered, but they knew it was time to call the police.

Once the authorities arrived, the digging at the site continued. As the workers pulled the bones from the soil, they noticed that they were small and fragile. With each new bone they uncovered, it became more and more clear that they had discovered the body of a child. The men had expected to find a single body—which would have been terrible enough. But as they continued to work, they made a terrible discovery: There wasn't just one body buried alongside the highway. There were *five* skeletons. And all of them children!

The workers were shaken. They could not believe that what had started as a typical workday was turning into a nightmare!

The grave where the children were buried was very shallow—only about two feet deep.

It looked as if whoever had buried the children might have been in a hurry to conceal the bodies. The sandy soil alongside the road made the grave easy to dig, but there were no explanations for how the children had gotten there. The police searched their records for any clues about missing children in the area, but there was no trace or reports of missing children.

The only clue left behind was a single, small, laced shoe—so lonely among the tiny bones. The sight of it made people mourn for these poor, unknown children. Locals thought maybe a family of early settlers had lost their children to a disease or some terrible accident, and in their sorrow, had buried them by the side of the road.

But maybe that wasn't the whole story.

Earlier that year, another eerie discovery had been made near Red Iron Lake and the five skeletons. It was another body! This skeleton was also small, but this time, the bones were tucked inside a wooden box. Just like the other skeletons, the identity of the remains was unknown.

It seemed the lake held many secrets—secrets it has kept to this day.

Though the remains of the five (or possibly more?) children were given a proper burial, some believe their spirits still roam the shores of Red Iron Lake. On quiet evenings, when the water is still and the moonlight dances on its surface, people swear they can hear the laughter of children playing by the lake. Some even claim to have seen small figures skipping rocks, their giggles echoing into the night. Perhaps in the afterlife they have discovered childhood joys they never got to experience in life.

Or . . . do the children remain at the lake because what was left of their earthly bodies was removed from their final resting places? Are they still seeking their roadside grave? Either way, one can only hope the spirits of the little ones can find the joy and peace in the afterlife that they never experienced while they were among the living.

The children's identities remain a mystery, but their restless spirits continue to play by the water's edge, forever a part of the haunted beauty of Red Iron Lake.

I Hope the Taku-He Stays Away from Me!

Many believe there is a massive man-like beast that lives in densely forested areas. The hairy creature walks on two legs and is tremendously powerful. This mysterious being goes by many different names. Some call it Sasquatch. Others call it Bigfoot. In South Dakota, it's called Taku-He.

Once you've seen this beast, you'll never forget it. Those who have encountered a

Taku-He have described it as between seven to nine feet tall. Its muscular body is covered with dark, coarse fur. The creature is said to reek of rotting flesh.

Those who have gotten a look at the terrible beast from the front say it has a large head with a flat face, small ears, and a sloping forehead that bulges out just above its glowing eyes. Witnesses report that these piercing eyes are red or yellow and can be seen at night. The creature is said to have long arms that reach below its knees and large hands with sharp claws.

And, of course, the Taku-He has big feet!

If this creature

sounds scary to you, just imagine encountering it while you are alone in the woods. That is exactly what happened to the residents of Little Eagle in Corson County in the 1970s.

It all began when Mrs. Phoebe Little Dog spotted the massive beast in a pasture near Little Eagle. She reported the sighting, but that was just the beginning. Before it was all over, Mrs. Little Dog reported seeing the Taku-He an amazing twenty-five times!

She wasn't the only resident of Little Eagle to encounter the creature. Cecelia Thunder Shield and Dan Uses Arrow were foraging for mushrooms when they encountered the beast. They trembled in silence as they observed the unknown creature with arms so long, they touched its ankles! Terrified, the local residents ran from the beast to the nearby home of Albert Dog.

The pair arrived at Albert's home breathless

from the run with their hearts racing in fear. They described what they had just seen to Albert, but there was little he could do besides offer them a cool drink and a place to rest as they recovered from the ordeal.

During that same time, neighbors started to hear eerie, high-pitched shrieks coming from deep in the woods. People sometimes described the sound as similar to an elephant trumpeting. The sound scared the residents of Little Eagle and agitated their pet dogs. When the shrieks began, dogs started to bark and

howl and nothing their owners did could calm them down.

The sightings continued, but they weren't taken too seriously. That is, until the beast was spotted near Little Eagle School. This time, the townspeople had had enough. It was one thing for the creature to scare adults, but no one was willing to risk the safety of the town's children.

Fourteen armed men and two officers from the Bureau of Indian Affairs banded together to find the beast. They headed into the woods. Some of the men were on horseback. Others

were riding all-terrain vehicles. All of them were determined to hunt down whatever was terrifying the town of Little Eagle.

The search offered some clues but not much else. The group discovered footprints far too large to be human near the river. And they did not match the footprints of any known animal. Witnesses recall that the footprints were eighteen inches long by eight inches wide. That is about the size of a skateboard! Some were certain they were looking at the footprints of a

Taku-He—a creature they'd believed was just a legend only a few days earlier!

The hunt ended at the river. Most of the search party agreed the beast had crossed the river and was gone. At least for now.

Days later, a bird hunter in the area discovered the body of a teenager at the bottom of a ravine. Although there was no proof, people assumed the Taku-He was the culprit. Later, a report came in of a massive beast chasing cows in a pasture. If the Taku-He had crossed the river, it appeared that the creature had returned.

Then, on October 4, 1977, a local teenager named Elvis Flying By went missing. After scouring the woods and finding nothing, the townspeople started to believe that the young man had had a deadly encounter with the Taku-He.

Later that same month, an elderly woman encountered the beast in her trailer park.

Mrs. Hanna Shooting Bear caught a glimpse of something strange as she passed by the window in her home. She went to the window to get a better look, and may have wished she hadn't! Right outside, plain as day, she saw a horrible, hairy creature peering into one of her neighbor's windows.

Mrs. Shooting Bear screamed in terror. Her neighbor heard the screaming, so he grabbed his rifle and rushed out the door of his home to help. It didn't take him long to discover the cause of all of the shouting. Standing in

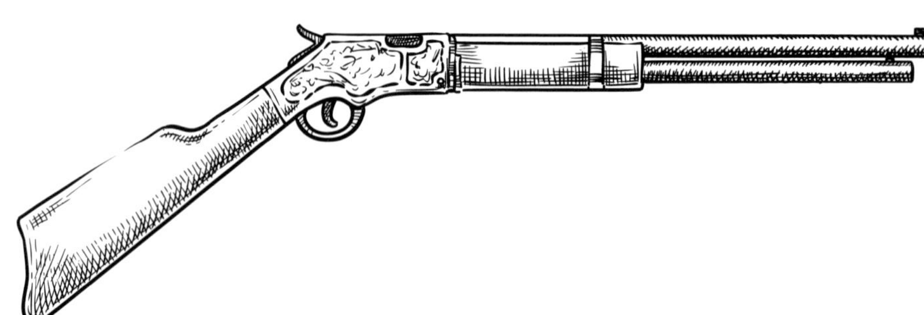

front of the man was a towering, hairy beast! Thinking fast, the man fired six shots into the air, hoping the sound would scare the beast away.

It worked. The beast fled. But the town was still no closer to finding the Taku-He.

In the years that followed, a group of teenagers went hiking in the nearby woods and never returned. Just like Elvis Flying By, the teens seemed to have disappeared without a trace. Since this happened in an area where Taku-He had been sighted, the beast was again blamed for the missing teens.

In April 1986, another group of teens narrowly escaped a similar fate. The group was in the Brown County Forest when they heard a sound that made their blood run cold. They could not see the source of the frightening, indescribable sounds, and they didn't want to stick around to find out where they were coming from.

The group ran as fast as they could away from the sound. When they eventually reached safety, they contacted the authorities. The teens didn't know what they had encountered in those woods, but they were certain whatever it was had meant to harm them.

If you think this is all in the past, guess again. According to *Ghosts and Legends of South Dakota* author Deborah A. Cuyle, there were nineteen reported Bigfoot sightings in South Dakota in 2023. And those are just from

the people brave enough to come forward. Imagine how many others have seen a strange creature in the forest and kept it to themselves for fear people would think they were foolish—or worse—liars!

How many sightings of the Taku-He will it take for people to finally believe the dangerous creature exists? In the town of Little Eagle, few doubt the beast lives among them. Do you have to see the Taku-He with your own eyes to believe in it? Or is the evidence there, but the truth too terrible to believe?

A Ghostly Goodbye

Thanks for exploring the spooky side of northeast South Dakota with us!

From the spooky Fort Sisseton to the lost children of Red Iron Lake, ghosts seem to be everywhere in South Dakota! All this ghost talk might have you hiding under the covers, hoping you will never encounter a ghost. Or maybe it has inspired you to begin your own paranormal investigations.

If you *do* decide to go exploring in hopes of having your own ghostly encounter, watch out! You just might get more than you bargained for. Ghosts that seem a little spooky in the book could be TERRIFYING in real life!

If you seek out the spirits for yourself, follow a few basic rules: Stick to places you are allowed to enter. Many people do not welcome ghost hunters on their property. If you get permission to seek out the spirits, make sure

your ghostly adventure is a safe one. Remember to stay in a group, take notes, and always—and I do mean ALWAYS —watch your back.

You never know just who, or what, might be right behind you!

Anna Lardinois tingles the spines of Milwaukee locals and visitors through her haunted, historical walking tours known as Gothic Milwaukee. The former English teacher is an ardent collector of stories, an avid walker, and a sweet treat enthusiast. She happily resides in a historic home in Milwaukee that, at this time, does not appear to be haunted.

Check out some of the other *Spooky America* titles available now!

Spooky America was adapted from the creeptastic *Haunted America* series for adults. *Haunted America* explores historical haunts in cities and regions across America. Here's more from the original *Ghosts and Legends of Northeast South Dakota* author, Deborah Cuyle:

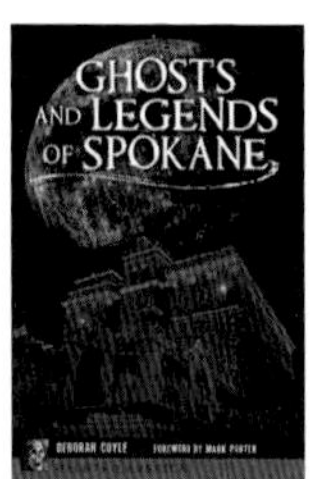